Dedication:
I dedicate this book to my great nieces, Autumn and Isla, and to my great nephew Grayson. Haw'aa for making me your Auntie Naanii! Dalang dii kuyaadang (I love you all).

Editors: Allison Parker and Emma Bullen
Text and illustration copyright © Medicine Wheel Education Inc. 2019
All rights reserved. Printed in PRC
ISBN: 978-1-9891221-9-8
For more information, visit us at www.medicinewheel.education

Gifts From Raven

Written by K̲ung Jaadee

Illustrated by Jessika von Innerebner

Gifts From Raven is an adaptation of K̲ung Jaadee's beautiful book, **Raven's Feast**, for a younger audience (ages 4-6). In order to make the story more accessible for this age group, the story has been shortened, simplified and given a rhyming scheme. This book was created with K̲ung Jaadee and has her enthusiastic approval, and we are excited to offer it to you.

Raven created the world brand new,
with forests of green and oceans of blue.
He made whales, bears and butterfly wings,
people and seashells and all other things.

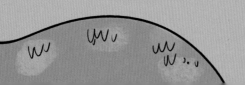

Raven also built houses all facing the sea,
made out of the wood of the red cedar tree.

He gathered berries and clams and he fished.
Then he dried them all out to eat when he wished.

The food he'd collected looked very appealing,
but it also gave Raven quite a lonely feeling.

He wished that he had other people to share the food and the houses and all that was there.

So he decided to host a very big feast,
for people from the North, South, West and East!

People arrived from every location,
and they were unique from nation to nation.

His guests shared their stories
and songs while they ate,
laughing and talking,
they all stayed up late.

When it was time for the guests to depart,
each left with a beautiful gift in their heart.

This gift was a talent that they each had inside,
a talent to share and never to hide.

Raven has given a gift to us all,
but it's up to us to hear it's call.

You might like to cook, or garden or dance,
so follow your talent and give it a chance.

Love yourself fully and let your light shine,
you embrace your gift and I'll embrace mine!

A fews words in Haida and how to say them

Yáahl (yaw-hl) – Raven

Ts'úu gid (ch-u-gid) – Red cedar

X̲aads nee (haw-ds nay) – house

Haw'aa (how-uh) - Thank you

Kung Jaadee (Roberta Kennedy) is a traditional Haida storyteller, singer and drummer form Haida Gwaii. She teaches Xaad Kil/ Haida language and culture and delights audiences at events across Canada.

She loves singing her traditional songs, laughing, drumming and learning her language. Her name was presented to her at her great uncle's memorial feast by her cousin, Crystal Robinson, and means "Moon Woman".

MEDICINE WHEEL EDUCATION

"...balm for the soul, enthralling, highly recommended..."
(Montreal Gazette)

"Raven causes magic...[Kung Jaadee's] compelling delivery keeps her audience enraptured
with these magical tales...a wonderful show, and perfect for two-leggeds of all ages."
(TheatreInLondon.ca)

"Four Stars"
(Saskatoon Star-Phoenix)

Kung Jaadee is a traditional Haida singer, drummer, and storyteller and one of Canada's leading aboriginal performers. She has performed at venues all over Canada including theatres, schools, universities, museums, libraries, conferences, festivals, community groups, and traditional feasts.

Kung Jaadee also gives workshops on topics related to storytelling, aboriginal culture, youth empowerment, and healing.

If you would like to book Kung Jaadee contact:

Email:
roberta@sharkhouse.ca

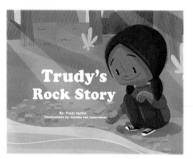

Books for ages 7-12 (available in English and French)

Educational lesson plans and posters available online!

The Eagle Feather
Written By Kevin Locke
Illustrated by Jessika von Innerebner

Gifts from Raven
Written by Kung Jaadee
Illustrated by Jessika von Innerebner

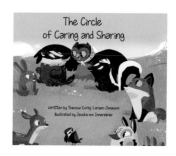

The Circle of Caring and Sharing
written by Theresa 'Corky' Larsen-Jonasson
illustrated by Jessika von Innerebner

Trudy's Healing Stone
Written by Trudy Spiller
Illustrated by Jessika von Innerebner

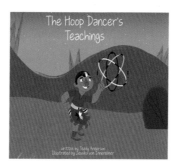

The Hoop Dancer's Teachings
Written by Teddy Anderson
Illustrated by Jessika von Innerebner

Phyllis's Orange Shirt

Books for ages 4-6 (available in English)

Contact us:
Address: 108-800 Kelly Road, Victoria, BC, V9B 6J9
Website: www.medicinewheel.education
Email: info@medicinewheel.education
Phone: 1-877-422-0212